100
CRA
FOR PRES

Here are 100 ideas for simple crafts based on simple concepts. Making their own creations will delight preschoolers—even if they require a little help from you. Some of these crafts are geared for 2 and 3 year olds, but most are for older preschoolers—those who can use scissors and follow simple directions. Some of these suggestions require advance preparation by an adult or adult assistance. To help you prepare for each craft, the materials needed are printed in bold type.

Don't forget to praise your preschoolers for the effort they put into their projects!

100 CRAFTS FOR PRESCHOOLERS

Published by David C. Cook Publishing Co.
850 N. Grove Ave.
Elgin, IL 60120
Cable Address: DCCOOK

Edited by Dave and Neta Jackson
Design: Christopher Patchel and Dawn Lauck

Printed in the United States of America

ISBN: 1-55513-140-9

CONTENTS

1 Fish and Net

In Bible times, fishermen used nets instead of poles to catch fish.

In advance: Cut out a cardboard **fish pattern**. Use a **felt-tip marker** to trace the fish pattern onto a sheet of **paper** for each child. Cut six **thin strips of paper** (11"-12" long) for each child. Use differents colors of paper to get a pretting effect. These strips will form a "fishing net."

Give each child a fish to cut out with blunt-edged **scissors**. Fish can then be glued onto sheets of **blue construction paper**. If desired, the edges of the blue paper can be torn slightly to create an illusion of water.

Then help children **glue** on strips of construction paper so that the strips overlap in a horizontal and vertical manner, giving the appearance of a net. (Some children may actually be able to weave the strips over and under with some assistance.) *Optional:* Glue on nylon net material or plastic vegetable nets if available.

2 Terrycloth Babies

Give each child a 6" square of **terrycloth**. Cut circles from **construction paper** and let children draw faces on circles, *or* cut baby faces from appropriate gift wrap. **Paste** a baby's face in one corner of each terrycloth square, then fold the other corners as if wrapping a real baby.

Use these little visual aides when you teach Bible stories involving babies—Samson, Isaac, Samuel, Moses, and Jesus.

3 Palm Branches

Give each child a piece of **green construction paper** and show how to fold it in half lengthwise. Then help children round off the two open corners with (blunt-edged) **scissors**. Children may cut slits along the open side, but they should be careful to leave some room between the slits and not to cut through the fold. Unfold for palm branches.

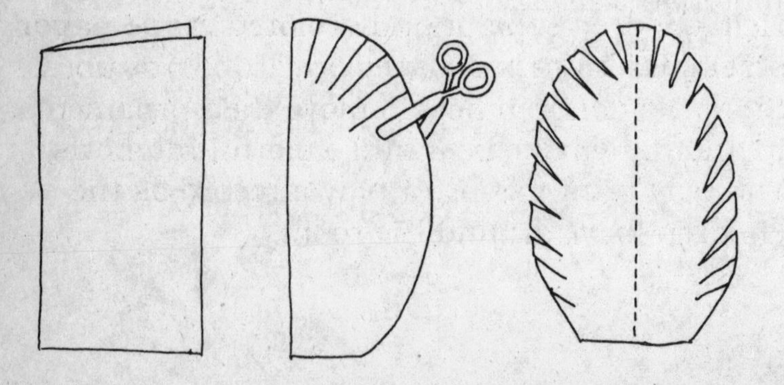

4 Kingly Crowns

You'll need:

- ❑ **lightweight cardboard**
- ❑ **aluminum foil**
- ❑ **stapler, glue**
- ❑ **glitter, sequins, etc.**

For each child, provide a strip of cardboard about 2" to 3" wide and long enough to wrap around child's head. Help children cover strips of cardboard by pasting or gluing large pieces of aluminum foil around them.

Decorate crowns with whatever materials you have available. If you add glitter and sequins, you may want them to dry a little before the children wear them. When ready, wrap the crown around the child's head. Staple or tape the ends together so the crowns will be the proper size for each child's head.

Crowns can be worn when acting out stories such as the kind king and the unforgiving servant.

5 Noah's Rainbow

Help children **tape** brightly colored **crepe paper streamers** to **paper plates** or cardboard tubes. Show the children how to move their ornaments in an arc to make beautiful, colorful rainbows. You may want to sing or play a record as the children move around the room.

6 King Solomon Figure

You'll need:

- ❑ **8 oz. white paper cup**
- ❑ **small Styrofoam ball**
- ❑ **toothpicks**
- ❑ **construction paper**
- ❑ **colored markers**
- ❑ **6" chenille wire**

In advance: Cut a construction paper crown to fit around the Styrofoam ball for each figure.

Give each child a 6-8 oz. white paper (or Styrofoam) cup, a chenille wire cut in half, a small Styrofoam ball, and a paper crown.

Have each child turn the cup upside down and color Solomon's robe on it with markers. Fashion arms from the chenille wire, folding the hands in front. **Tape** or staple them to the sides of the cup.

Child can then draw a face on the Styrofoam ball. Child may want to decorate the crown with **sequins** or glitter before you glue or staple it onto the head. Finally, attach the head to the cup by bringing two or three toothpicks up through the open end of the cup, punching them through the closed end, and up into the Styrofoam ball.

7 Camels

You'll need:

- ❑ **unwaxed paper cups**
- ❑ **brown paper**
- ❑ **brown yarn**
- ❑ **markers, crayons, tape**

In advance: Cut out camel heads and four 3" strips from brown paper for each set of legs. Draw eyes, mouth, and nose on both sides of each head with a marker.

Give children plain unwaxed paper cups. Let them scribble color on the cups.

Turn cups upside down and help children tape on the camel head and four legs. Bend the legs back as if the camel is kneeling. Tape on brown yarn for a tail.

Have children pretend to ride camels with their fingers. Tell how the wise men rode a long way on their camels to worship baby Jesus.

8 Sheep

You'll need:

- ❑ **empty spools**
- ❑ **cotton balls**
- ❑ **chenille wires**
- ❑ **glue**

In advance: Collect empty spools. Prepare sheep base by putting three chenille wires through the spool. Twist the wires together at either end of the spool. Bend four "feet" down; cut the other wire shorter for head and tail. Be sure to have a finished example for the children to look at.

Provide a spool, cotton balls, and glue for each child. Show children how to drop glue on a cotton ball. Place the cotton ball on the spool and hold for a moment to secure. Cover front, back, top, and sides. Place one cotton ball on top of the neck wire. Glue a second ball to that one and shape into a head. Cut small construction paper circles for eyes and ears, and glue onto head.

9 Creation Mobile

Provide each child with a **wire coat hanger** and four or five 2-3" **circles** cut from tagboard. (If you can obtain them, small, lightweight plastic lids used for take-out beverages would be ideal for this project.) In the center of each circle, have preschoolers place a **sticker** of something God has created—a flower, tree, bird, animal, the sun, or a person. Or, children can cut out small pictures from magazines and glue them onto the circles.

Preschoolers will need assistance with the rest of this project. Poke small holes at the top of the circles. Put **thread** through each hole; knot it; then, tie the other end of the string to the bottom of the hanger. Vary the lengths of the threads to give the mobile an interesting appearance.

Children can hang these in their bedrooms as reminders of what God has made.

10 People Puppets

Cut out the inside circle from **paper plates**. Have children make faces on the paper circles, then **paste** the heads to **craft sticks**.

For Bible characters: Have children color hair, beards, or head shawls depending on the story.

For working people: Cut out **construction paper** hats representing different kinds of jobs. Have children paste hats on the heads. Use the puppets to act out people working.

11 Sad-and-Glad Puppets #1

Provide each child with two **small paper plates** and a wooden **craft stick**. Let children draw sad faces on one of their plates and happy faces on the other. Provide **yarn** to **glue** around the faces for hair. Have children glue the plates back to back with the stick secured in between to form a handle.

Children can hold up the appropriate face as you tell stories of someone who does something wrong . . . then tells God, "I'm sorry."

12 Sad-and-Glad Puppets #2

Make sad-and-glad puppets from **small paper bags** with fold-over ends. Draw a smiling face on fold-down end. Put body on rest of bag. Under flap, draw sad face. When bag is open, puppet is sad. Bring flap down to make puppet smile.

13 Sad-and-Glad Puppets #3

Give each child a piece of plain **paper**, a circle of paper for a face, a half circle (a little larger) for hair, and a **paper fastener** for a nose.

Help the child fasten the circle to the plain paper by pushing the fastener through the center of both. The child may draw two eyes on the circle (the eyes and paper-fastener nose must be in a straight line).

Help the child put **paste** only on the curved edge of the semicircle. Lay the semicircle over the circle, being careful not to let the paste touch the face circle. Let the child draw on a smile. Turn the face circle so the smile disappears beneath the hair. Let the child draw a mouth with the corners turned down.

As you tell a story, children can make the expressions on the face match story characters.

14 Flannelboard

Children can make their own flannel boards and flannelgraph pieces. For each child cut a piece of **cardboard** 8 1/2" x 11" and a piece of plain **flannel** slightly larger. Help them **glue** the material to the cardboard. Figures of Jesus and disciples from old **teaching pictures** or people cut from magazines can be backed with construction paper. Glue a small piece of **felt** or sandpaper on the back and the figures will stick to the board. Attach an **envelope** to the back of the board to hold the figures. Be sure child's name is on the board.

15 Making a Church

Help preschoolers make their own church buildings from boxes. Give each child the **bottom of a small box**. Provide a **pointed paper cup** for each or a cone shape made from a circle of paper. Children may cover the boxes with white paper if desired. Have children turn their boxes upside down and color the windows and a door, then **tape** the cups or cones on the box bottoms (now the tops) for steeples.

This craft is a good visual for talking about why we come to church and things we can do to take care of God's house.

16 Chenille Wire People

Man or woman: Use two **chenille wires**. With one wire, make the head and arms. Fasten the second wire to the first at the neck. Shape the second wire into the body and legs.
Child: Use only one long chenille wire and shape as for adult, only smaller.
Robe: Cut a hole in the center of a piece of fabric 8" x 3". Fit over figure's head; wrap **string** or a rubber band around figure's waist.
Shawl: Cut a piece of fabric 1 1/2" x 7" in size. Drape it over figure's head, allowing one end to hang down in front. Bring the other end across the front and over the opposite shoulder so it hangs down in back. Fasten in place with a **small safety pin**.

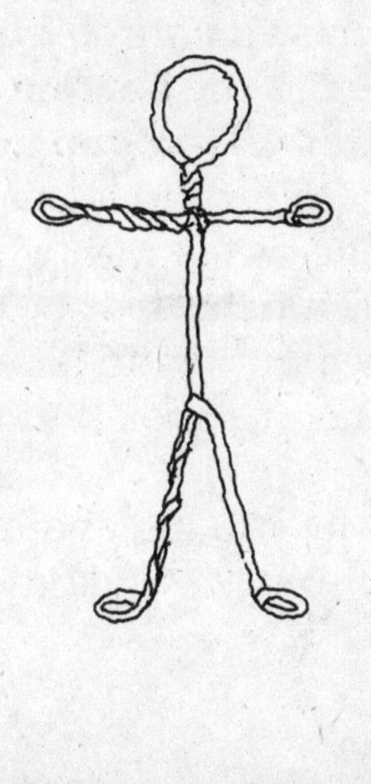

17 Chenille Wire Animals

To make a basic animal, use one **chenille wire** for the head and forelegs. Fasten a second wire to the first at the neck and shape this second wire into the body, hind legs, and tail.

For a lamb, **glue cotton balls** onto the body.

For a donkey, use three wires. The first makes the head and ears; the second makes the fore-legs and body; the third makes the hind legs and tail.

A giraffe also requires three wires, one for the head and neck, a second for the forelegs, and a third for the body and hind legs.

For an elephant, use four wires. The first makes the trunk and head, the second makes the body, the third makes the forelegs, and the fourth, hind legs.

18 Friendship Paper Dolls

In advance: Fold sheets of **white construction paper** in thirds, like a fan. Cut a simple doll cutout so that when the page is open there are three figures holding hands.

Give one set of figures to each child to color. Then, help children **tape** their figures all around the room, joining them together at the hands.

19 Flower Pictures

In advance: Cut three flower stems from **green construction paper** and a square of **red construction paper** (about 5" x 5") for each picture.

Give each child a sheet of construction paper, three flower stems, three pieces of **facial tissue**, and a red square. Help children glue the flower stems in the middle of the paper. **Punch** a hole at the top of the flower stems. Twist the facial tissue at the center and pull through the hole from front to back about one inch. **Tape** to the back of the construction paper. Place the square of red paper over the bottom of the stems to look like a flowerpot. Hang the pictures all around the room.

20 Self-Portrait Figures

Give children figures cut from **heavy paper** or tagboard to decorate as self-portraits. Children can decorate the figures by coloring them with **crayons** or marking pens to reflect each child's own hair, skin color, and clothing. If you wish, bring in some small **mirrors** so that children can look at their own personal features. *Optional:* Add scraps of yarn for hair and fabric scraps for clothing.

Enjoy how special and different each portrait is—just like each child is special and different.

21 Neighborhood Mural

Put up a long piece of **butcher paper** or newsprint. Invite adults from the church to work with the children. Have the adults cut out pictures of people, houses, and other buildings from **magazines** or out of colored paper. Have children draw details such as trees and streets, and **glue** the pictures on the mural. The mural can actually represent the surrounding neighborhood.

Write "Our Neighborhood" on the mural. Hang the mural in the church hall for everyone to see. Hang the mural low enough so that the children can admire their work.

22 Star Designs

Give each child a precut **cardboard star** and a piece of **drawing paper**. Have children place their star patterns underneath their papers. Then have them color over the stars to make a textured design as the star shapes appear. Interesting patterns will appear as the star designs overlap. These can be used as a background for a Christmas scene.

23 Paper Chain Christmas Tree

Give each child several **4" strips of paper** and show how to make a chain by taping the ends of one of the strips together to make a circle, then interlock a second strip of paper to make another circle, until the desired length is reached. **Thumbtack** the chains to a bulletin board so the final result is a triangular Christmas tree. Use a square of **brown construction paper** for a base and **white construction paper** for snow.

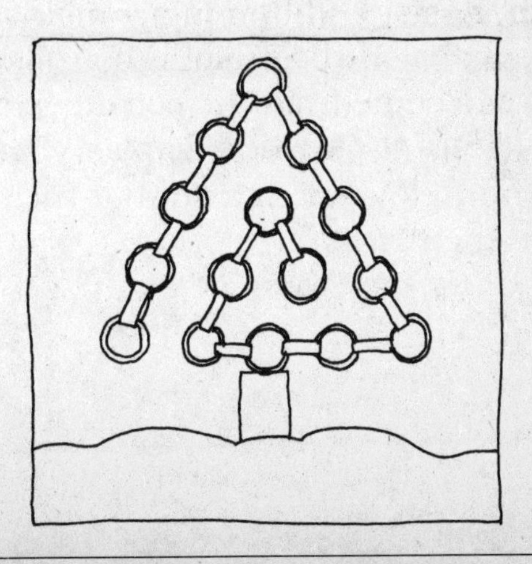

24 Easter Tree

In advance: Prepare a large paper tree, using **green paper**, and attach it to the wall or bulletin board. Also prepare large egg shapes from **colored paper**.

Let each child decorate one or more of the egg shapes, using **crayons**, **glue** and **glitter**, and **sticker stars**. Children may **tape** their egg shapes to the tree in any position they wish.

25 Thank You, God

In advance: Fashion a large cornucopia from **brown paper** and mount it on the bulletin board.

Provide children with large **paper plates**. Let children draw on the plates the favorite things that they're **thankful** for, or let them paste pictures of those things that they've cut from magazines. If they wish, have them decorate their plates with designs, **stickers, colorful leaves**, or **fabric trim**. Assist children in arranging their "thankful" plates on the bulletin board so that they appear to come from the cornucopia.

Cut out letters to title this display "Thank You, God, for . . ."

26 'Special Things' Picture

You'll need:
- ❑ **large piece of construction paper or tagboard**
- ❑ **pictures from magazines**
- ❑ **a picture of Jesus**
- ❑ **a picture of each child's family**

Have children cut pictures of "special things" from magazines. **Paste** the picture of Jesus in the middle of the large piece of paper. Paste the other pictures carefully to the newspaper. It's okay if they overlap, but don't cover the picture of Jesus.

Children can hang these in their bedrooms to remind them of who and what is special to them.

27 Flowers

Let children make flowers to represent the people who help them.

Cut four petals in one shape like a double figure 8 from **construction paper**. Paste two of these on a **craft stick.** Make several of these flowers. Print the names of helpers on the petals or stems: Father, Mother, Brother, Sister, Teacher, Mail Carrier, Police Officer, etc. "Plant" these flowers in **Styrofoam** or clay in a **spray can lid** or a margarine tub. Put "Thank You" on the flower pot.

28 Church Banks

Give each child a sheet of **construction paper** and an **envelope**. **Paste** the the envelope with the flap up onto paper. Decorate the envelope to resemble a church: With **crayons** or markers, draw a door and windows on the bottom section of the envelope; draw a cross above the pointed tip of the flap. Children may keep next Sunday's offering money in their "banks."

29 Jesus Mobile

Make a 2 1/2" circle on **white paper** for each child. Draw a 1 1/2" circle inside the 2 1/2" circle. Cut out the center so that you will have a ring. Use the center to make a 1" circle.

Print the Bible verse, "I believe that you are the Son of God—John 11:27," on the bottom of the ring. Let children color the ring.

Print the word "Jesus" on one side of the 1" circle. Give each of child a **sticker picture of Jesus** to place on the other side of the 1" circle.

Punch a hole in the top of the 1" circle and near the top and bottom edge of the top of the ring. Thread with a length of knotted **yarn**. Children can hang this mobile in their bedroom to remind them that Jesus is the Son of God.

30 Church Building

You'll need:

- ❑ **empty fast-food hamburger box for each child**
- ❑ **construction paper; chenille wires**
- ❑ **stickers of Jesus; glue**

Help children cut windows and doors from paper. Glue door on the side of the hamburger box that opens. Glue windows on other sides. Cut chenille wire into two 3" pieces. Twist two wire pieces together to make a cross. Glue cross to top of church near door. Open the box and attach a sticker of Jesus inside.

31 Thank-You God

Discuss how God made each of us the same—two eyes, a nose, etc. Then discuss how God made each of us different—hair color, size, abilities, etc.

Give each child an 18" **chenille wire**. Show them how to bend and twist it to make the head, body, and legs of a stick-figure person. Add a 6" chenille wire for arms. Staple the figure onto a piece of **construction paper** with the title "God created me. Thank You, God."

32 God's Care Button

In advance: Lightly print "God cares for me" around the inner top edge of a **small paper plate**. Let the children cut off the outside border of the plate so only the center with the printing remains. Then have them trace over the penciled words with a crayon.

Give each child a **happy face sticker** to place on the circle under the words. Then attach a **small safety pin** to the back of the circle with **tape** to pin their buttons to their shirts or dresses.

33 Sun Catcher

You'll need:

- ❑ **circles precut from white construction paper**
- ❑ **different colors of tissue paper**
- ❑ **paste; yarn; hole punch**
- ❑ **alternative: one plastic lid per child**

Give each child a white circle. Place a few sheets of brightly colored tissue paper in the center of the table. Show the children how to tear off a small piece of tissue paper and paste it to the circle. Let the children continue decorating their circles. (*Alternative:* Paste pieces of tissue paper on plastic lids.)

When the project is dry, make a hole in the top; tie a piece of yarn through it. Hang the sun catchers in a window or from the ceiling. The sun catcher can be a reminder that God made beautiful colors for us to enjoy!

34 Stained Glass Windows

You'll need:
- ❑ **lightweight cardboard**
- ❑ **black construction paper**
- ❑ **light colored chalk or crayon**
- ❑ **small scraps of brightly colored paper**

In advance: Make a stained glass window pattern (a rectangle with an arching top) from lightweight cardboard. Draw a 1" border around the inside of the pattern; cut out the area inside the border.

Give each child a sheet of black construction paper. Help children trace around the outside and inside edges of the window pattern with a light-colored crayon or chalk. Help children cut along the *outside* edges of their windows. Let children choose a variety of precut scraps of colored paper—or let them tear their own shapes. Children can **glue** the scraps on the window in a mosiac design, leaving the border as a window frame.

These windows can help remind children that Sunday is a special day to worship God.

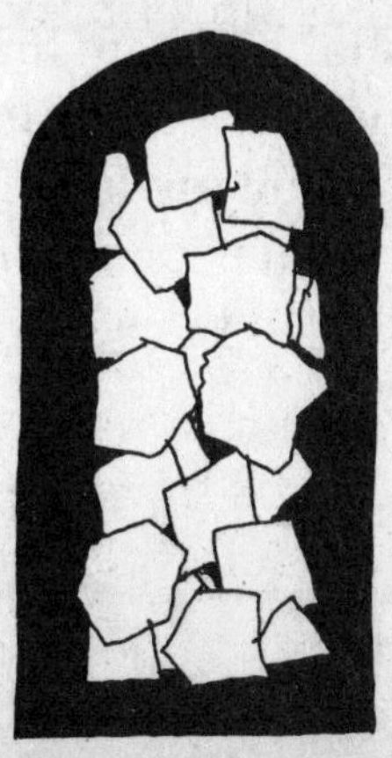

35 Happy Faces

You'll need:

- ❑ **paper plates or precut paper circles**
- ❑ **small paper circles and semicircles**
- ❑ **paste or tape; yarn**
- ❑ **wooden tongue depressors or craft sticks**
- ❑ **optional: several mirrors**

Give each child a paper plate or precut paper circle to be a face. Also, provide each child with smaller paper circles to paste on for the eyes and nose. (*Option:* Let children look in mirrors as you point out where their facial features are located.) Paste the semicircles on the paper plates to make smiles. Use yarn to make hair. Tape or paste a wooden tongue depressor or craft stick to the back to make handles.

Happy faces can be used when singing songs of praise to God.

36 My Home and Family

Give each child a sheet of **construction paper**; position it horizontally. Cut off the upper corners to make a house shape. Draw lines to make a roof and four rooms. On each picture print the words, "I thank God for my family."

Let children draw their own families in their houses and tell why they're glad for their family.

37 Self-Portraits

Tape large sheets of **butcher paper** or newsprint to the floor. Have children take turns lying down on the paper and let other children trace around the bodies of their friends with **crayons**. Then have children color in the outlines of their friends to make life-size self-portraits. Put another sheet of paper behind each figure that has been colored and cut out front and back pieces. Children can also color the back pieces. Then **staple** fronts to backs and stuff with **crumpled newspaper**.

Line up the portraits. Look at all the friends who worked together! Guide children to thank God for their friends.

38 Praise Wall Hanging

In Bible times, important people, priests, and kings wore clothes made from purple cloth. Purple cloth was also used in the temple.

In advance: Print the words "We Praise God" on pieces of **purple construction paper**, one for each child.

Have children **glue yarn** or sprinkle glitter on the letters. Fold the top of the paper back one ince. Lay an 18" piece of yarn in the fold and glue or staple the folded flap down; tie the yarn for hanging. Cut the bottom of the construction paper to make fringe.

39 Snowflakes

Give each child a square of **white paper**, 5" x 5". Help child fold square into a triangle, then again, then again. With blunt **scissors**, child can cut nicks into the sides of the folded triangle. Unfold. Hang snowflakes in a window with a piece of **tape**, or attach a length of white thread to the top of the snowflake and tape the other end of the thread to the top of the window frame.

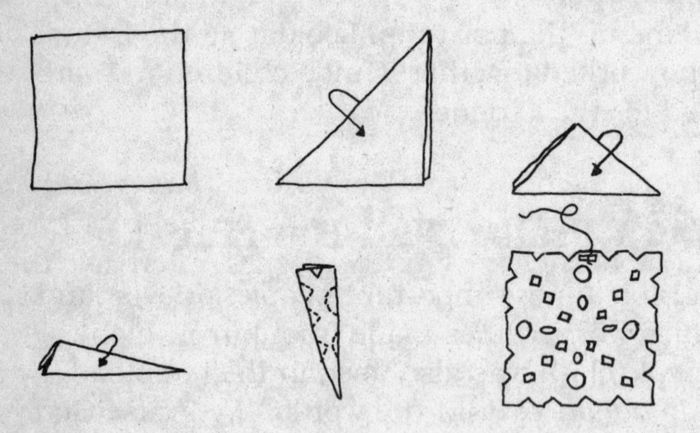

40 Bird Feeder #1

Cut a large opening on each side of a **quart milk carton**. Close the carton at the top and **punch** a hole in the peak. Fasten **cord** through the hole to tie the feeder to a tree branch. Let children put **sunflower seeds** and **bread crumbs** in it. Hang bird feeder on a low tree branch outside a window where children can see it.

41 Bird Feeder #2

Help children fill spaces between **pine cone** scales with **peanut butter**, then sprinkle **bird seed** or bread crumbs on it. If you do not have pine cones, use a sheet of cardboard. Spread peanut butter on the cardboard and sprinkle bird seed on it. Attach a string for hanging the feeder on a tree.

As you work, talk about the fact that birds often have a hard time finding food in winter, and that God is glad when we give them something to eat.

42 Pussy Willows

Give each child a sheet of **colored paper**. Help child draw several brown or black lines, which will be branches of pussy willows. Then give the child a number of small pieces of **cotton** to **paste** on the branches for pussy willow buds.

If possible, provide several real pussy willows for children to look at and touch.

43 Tulip

1. Fold a 4" square of red **paper** diagonally so that the opposite corners meet to form a triangle.
2. Fold the right corner of the triangle as shown.
3. Fold the left corner of the triangle as shown.
4. Fold the corners toward the back.
5. **Glue** or tape the tulip near the top of a sheet of **construction paper**.
6. Draw a stem and leaves with **markers**.

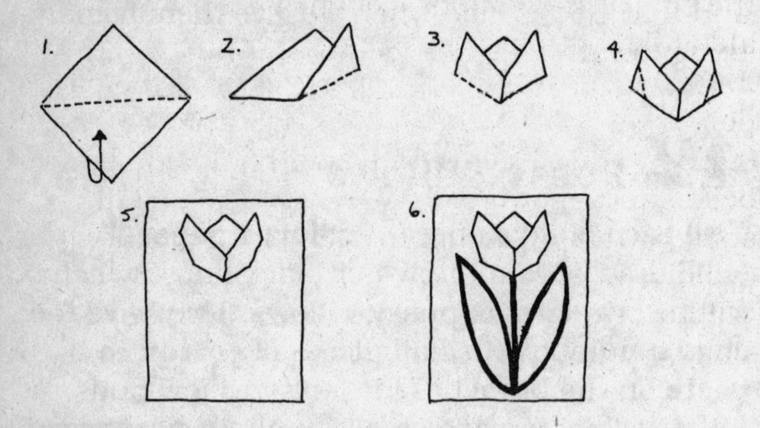

44 Autumn Trees

Provide each child with a simple tree cut from brown or black **construction paper**. **Paste** tree to piece of paper in a contrasting color. Show children how to tear or cut fall leaves from yellow, red, and orange paper strips. One method: Help children cut heart shapes from the paper, turning the hearts upside down to look like leaves. (*Option:* Bring in real leaves.) Children may paste or tape their leaves to the tree branches.

45 'Growing' Flowers

In advance: For each child, cut out (1) three bell shapes from **bright-colored paper** for flowers; (2) three green stems; and (3) a yellow circle for a sun. Place a large sheet of construction paper horizontally and cut three slits (the size of the stems) in it, about 2" from the bottom and 4" apart.

1. Give each child the construction paper prepared in advance; position it horizontally with the slits at the bottom. Let child color grass along the bottom.
2. **Paste** the sun in an upper corner of the paper.
3. Show children how to paste the upside-down bell shapes (flowers) to the top of each stem; stick bottom of stem into each slit and pull down.
4. Show child how the flower can "grow" by slowly pulling up on the flower.

46 Autumn Picture

You'll need:

- ❑ **pressed autumn leaves**
- ❑ **construction paper**
- ❑ **clear plastic wrap**
- ❑ **tape, scissors, string**

Let each child select a large, colorful autumn leaf and tape it on construction paper. Help child tape a piece of clear plastic wrap over the leaf to keep it from falling off. Then frame picture with strips of construction paper. Tape a loop of string to the top or back and child will have a nature picture ready to hang.

47 Spring Appreciation

Give each child a 9" x 12" piece of **green construction paper** folded in half horizontally. Help child cut through the fold, extending the cuts from the fold to an inch away from the opposite edge. Make cuts about 1/2" apart all along the fold to resemble grass.

The let each child draw several tulip shapes with stems on **colored construction paper**. Be sure to leave a 1" border at the bottom of each stem connecting all the tulip shapes. After the children cut out the flowers, position the border along the uncut edge of the grass and help them roll the grass and flowers together. The grass should be on the outside with the flowers sticking out of the top. **Tape** the edges so that the grass will not unroll.

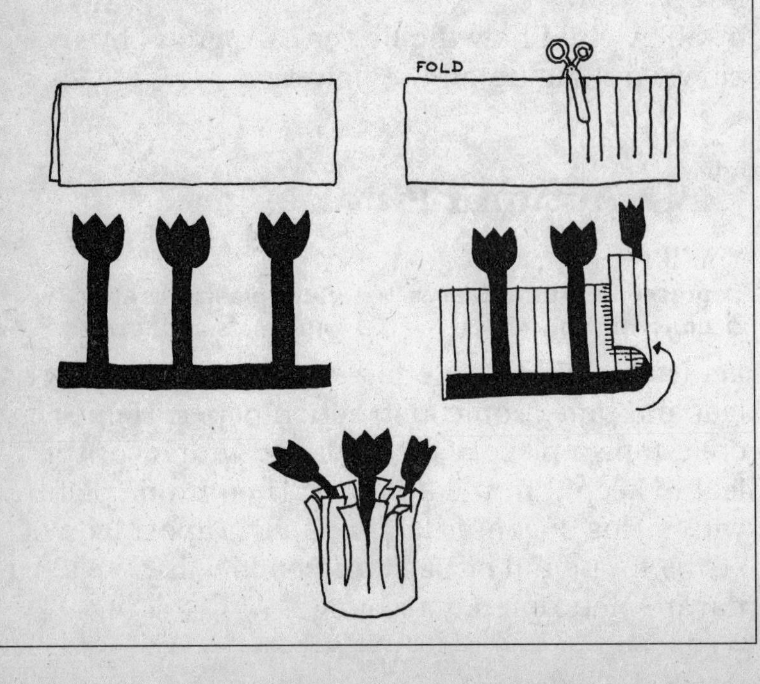

48 'Jesus Loves You' Basket

Show children how to . . .

1. Lick the flap shut on a **business-size envelope**.
2. Fold the envelope in half lengthwise.
3. Beginning on one side, cut away the open edges halfway down the length of the envelope to make a pretty handle (see illustration). Unfold.
4. Decorate the basket and handle with **crayons**, **stickers**, **glitter**, **sequins**, etc. Print "Jesus Loves You" on one side.
5. Spread apart the sides of the envelope to open up basket.
6. Fill the basket with treats (candy or flowers) and give to a friend. Tell your friend that Jesus loves him or her and you do, too!

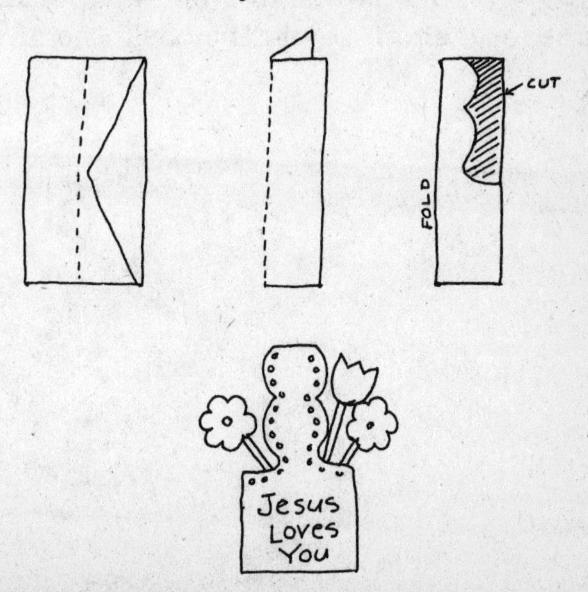

49 Bookmarks

Child can make several bookmarks to give as gifts to family members to put in their Bibles.

Provide **construction paper strips** about 1 1/2 by 5 inches.

Let child place a **sticker seal** of Jesus at the top of each strip. At the bottom, print "Jesus loves (Mother, Daddy, Becky)" to personalize each bookmark. For more durable bookmarks, cover the fronts and backs with a clear adhesive-backed plastic.

50 Gift Baskets

Give each child an empty **cottage cheese** or **margarine container**. Cover the outside with colorful **tissue paper**; **tape** or glue in place and attach a self-stick **bow**. Children may put **fruit**, **crayons**, or a **small toy** in the basket to give as a gift.

51 Sponge-Painted Tray

You'll need:

- ❑ **fiber vegetable trays or egg carton tops**
- ❑ **spring-type clothespins**
- ❑ **sponges; tempera paint; aluminum muffin tins**

Each child will need a fiber vegetable tray (ask at the produce department of the grocery store) or a fiber egg-carton top. (Do not use Styrofoam since tempera will not adhere properly.)

Cut "holey" sponges into 1 1/2" pieces. Clip a clothespin to each sponge piece. Pour a small amount of tempera paint into aluminum muffin tins. Let child dip the sponge into the paint and dab it on the tray. Provide each child with one sponge for each color, otherwise the paint will become muddy. Allow the trays to dry thoroughly.

Discuss things that could be kept in the tray: crayons, jewelry, pencils, odds and ends.

52 Carnations

For each flower, cut **facial tissues** into four 4"-diameter circles. Place a **button** on the center of the circles; thread a knotted yarn through the button and layers of tissue. Pull **yarn** through a slit in a **sheet of paper**; **tape** yarn down on the back of the paper. Then crumple each layer of tissue around the button. Draw a stem and leaves with a crayon. (*Option:* Spray perfume on the flowers.) Children can make the flowers to lonely or ill friends.

53 Vase and Flowers

You'll need:

- ❑ **empty spool**
- ❑ **lace or ribbon**
- ❑ **3 toothpicks; glue**
- ❑ **construction paper**

In advance: Cut three small flower shapes from construction paper for each child. Print the word "I" on one flower, "AM" on the next flower, and "SORRY!" on the third flower.

Show children how to glue ribbon or lace around the middle of the spool. Place a small amount of glue on the end of each toothpick and allow children to stick it on their flowers. A small wad of paper should be placed in each spool before arranging the "flowers."

The gift can be given to a friend or a family member when the child needs to say, "I'm sorry."

54 Paper Bag Basket

Cut 5" off the open end of a **lunch bag** for each basket. Let child decorate the sides of the bag with designs, using construction **paper scraps**, **glue**, and **crayons**. Help child use **scissors** to make a scalloped edge along the top of the bag.

Cut a strip from the discarded top of the paper bag, about 1 1/4" wide and 12" long. Tape to the sides of the decorated basket for a handle. Fill with **flowers, peanuts, candies**, or a **small gift** to give to a friend.

55 Get Well Pockets

In advance: Cut **paper plates** in half. Provide each child with a whole paper plate and one of the halves. Let each child decorate the plates (front side of whole plate; back side of half plate) with **crayon** designs. Write "Get Well Soon!" on the container.

Staple a half plate to a whole plate to make a pocket container. **Punch** a hole at the top and lace **yarn** through each plate so it can hang on the wall.

Explain that a sick friend or relative can use the pocket for tissues, a pad of paper and a pencil to write notes, or to keep get-well cards in.

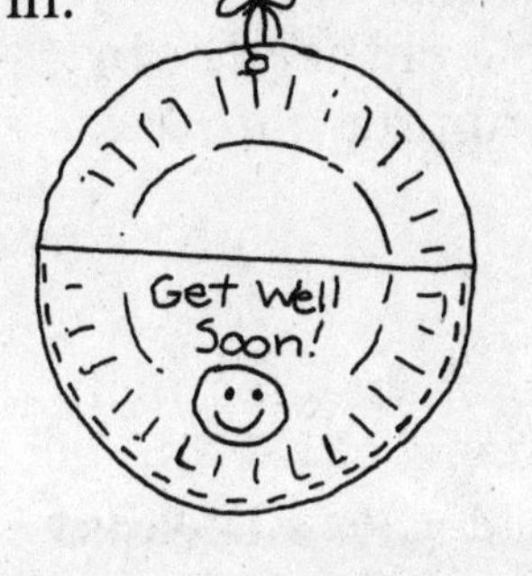

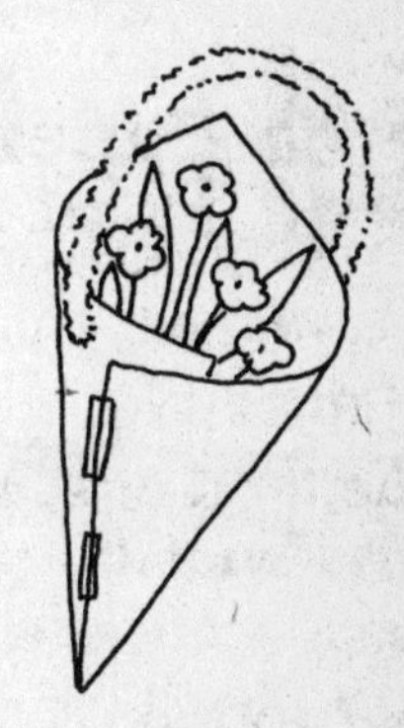

56 Cone Baskets

Let children scribble color a piece of **construction paper**. Roll the paper into cone shapes and **staple** or tape the sides to make a basket. **Tape** a **chenille wire** handle on each basket. Let the children put things in their baskets, such as **wild flowers** or small **plastic bags** filled with **nuts** and **raisins**, to give to a special person.

57 Christmas Paperweight

You'll need:

- ❑ **baby food jars**
- ❑ **stones to fill jars**
- ❑ ***optional*: glitter, wrapping paper**
- ❑ **construction paper**
- ❑ **paste or glue**

Give each child a red or green paper rectangle cut to fit around a baby food jar. Let child paste on scraps of torn construction paper to decorate the rectangle. (*Option:* Glue on glitter or small pictures cut from wrapping paper.)

After decorating the paper rectangle, paste it around the baby food jar. Fill the jar with small stones—be careful not to break the jar. Have preschoolers give this paperweight as a Christmas gift to grandparents or friends.

Vary this gift idea for any time of the year by decorating the paperweight in appropriate ways.

58 Photo Gift

In advance: Take **pictures of each child** and get them developed. Print "Happy Mother's Day," or other appropriate words, at the top of a sheet of **construction paper**. **Punch** holes about 1" apart around entire paper. Cut pieces of **yarn** 1 1/2 yards long. Wrap **masking tape** around yarn ends so it will go through holes easily.

Have children **glue** their photographs under the writing on their papers, and write their names underneath. Starting at the top, center, show them how to thread yarn in and out through the holes around the outside of the papers. Tie ends in a bow at top.

59 Gift Sachets

Sachets can be hung in closets to make clothes smell nice.

Give each child a sheet of **green or red construction paper** measuring 2 x 4 inches. Guide children in folding the paper in half; **staple** the sides closed. Help children sprinkle a few drops of **perfume** or cologne on a **cotton ball**. (Children might want to make two sachets—one using perfume for mother and the other using after-shave for father.) Place the cotton ball inside the sachet pocket.

With a **paper punch**, punch a hole at the top of the sachet through the front and back sides. Loop a piece of **yarn** through the hole and tie the sachet closed. Tie the ends of the yarn to make a loop so that the sachet can be hung up. **Stickers** can be added to the front and back of the sachet for decoration.

60 Butterfly Bookmarks

For each butterfly bookmark, provide a 1" x 7" strip of colored construction paper and a simple butterfly shape cut from white paper. Print the words "I love you" on the strip of colored **construction paper**.

Cover the worktable with **newspaper**. Let children color their butterflies, then help them spread a thin coat of **glue** on the butterfly and sprinkle **glitter** on the glue. Shake the butterfly gently over the newspaper to remove the excess glitter. Glue the butterfly to one end of the strip of paper.

61 Father's Day Gift Ideas

Scribble pictures. Children may scribble-color pictures on **drawing paper** and paste **black paper strips** around them to make a frame.
Pencil cans. Cut heavy **gift-wrap paper** or adhesive-backed shelf paper to fit around **empty soup cans** (be sure there are no sharp edges); **tape** in place.
Paper weights. Children can make paper weights by painting **rocks** with **tempera paint**. Let rocks dry; show how to make designs with a different color. **Shellac** if possible.

62 Hand Plaques

Roll out **play dough** or clay 1/2" thick in a colorful **paper plate**. Press child's hand into the clay to make imprint. Place a **ribbon** on the back of the plate for hanging purposes. When dry, place each plaque in a **paper bag** and tie a ribbon around the top of the bag. These can be given as presents for mother or father.

63 My Book . . . for You

Give children **crayons** and some sheets of **paper**. Have them draw several pictures of a sun, tree, flower, bird, family, house, pets, toys.

When drawings are finished, stack them neatly. Put a fresh sheet of paper on the top and on the bottom to make a cover. **Staple** books along the side. Or punch two holes in the book and tie together with yarn. Write "MY BOOK by . . ." and child's name on the cover.

Grandmother would love to receive this gift!

64 Place Mats

Help children weave place mats by putting narrow strips of **construction paper** or wallpaper in and out of slits cut evenly in a different colored sheet of construction paper.

65 Snowman I

You'll need:

- ❑ **marshmallows**
- ❑ **toothpicks**
- ❑ **Styrofoam square**
- ❑ **raisins**

Give each child three marshmallows and a Styrofoam square. Show children how to make snowmen by sticking the marshmallows together with toothpicks. Put two marshmallows together with one toothpick. Stick another toothpick halfway into the bottom marshmallow, then place the third marshmallow on this toothpick. Stick a third toothpick into the Styrofoam base and push the snowman onto the toothpick, so the snowman will stand. Two more toothpicks can be used for arms sticking out of the middle marshmallow. Use pieces of toothpicks to add raisin eyes and mouth to the top marshmallow.

66 Snowman II

Use a **paper plate** to make this happy snowman! Draw a line around the perimeter of the plate, 1" from the outer rim, leaving a 2" section blank at the top. Now draw another circle 2" inside the first one; leave a 2" section blank on this line as well, directly *opposite* from the first blank section. Cut along the lines. Do not cut where the blank sections are.

After cutting, you will have three sections: one solid circle in the middle and two hollow circles on the outside. All three sections will be connected by the uncut sections. Fold the solid center section up to form the head. Fold the outside hollow circle down to form the lower part of the snowman's body. The middle hollow circle will form the middle of the snowman's body. Decorate the top circle with **construction paper** features and a hat and scarf.

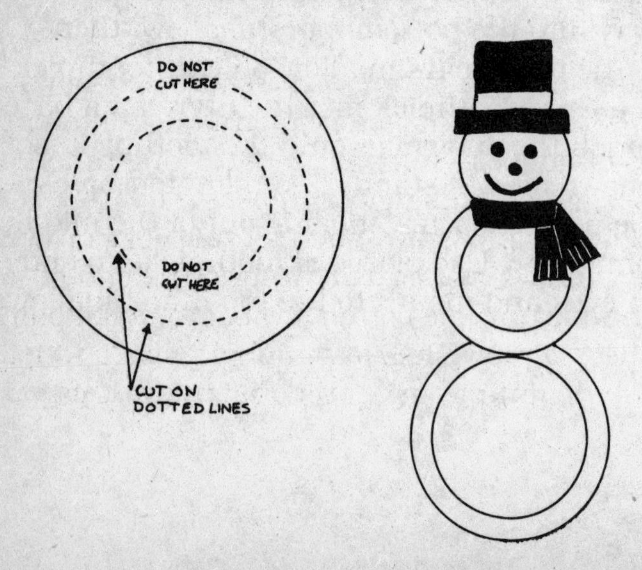

67 Finger Painting Fun

Preschoolers will love the feel and effect of making things in paint with their fingers. Provide **smocks** from old shirts to protect their clothes, and cover the work surface with **newspapers**. Be sure to dip the **paper** in **water** before you put paint on the paper. Help children use their fingers and hands in various ways to make different things in their pictures.

Here's a recipe for **finger paint** or it can be purchased at a craft or toy store:

1. Mix 1 1/2 cups cold-water starch with 1 1/2 cups soap flakes.
2. Slowly stir in 2 cups of cold water, stirring until the mixture is smooth and thick.
3. Add powdered tempera paint to make the colors you choose.

68 House Painting

Children enjoy painting pictures of their houses. Or they might like to paint pictures of different kinds of houses—tall apartments, long ranch houses, grass huts, igloos, tepees, etc.

Use washable paint, such as **tempera** or even finger paint. Twist **cotton** around the end of **toothpicks** (or use cotton swabs) to make paintbrushes. Dip brushes in tempera paint and let children paint pictures on **construction paper**.

69 My Own Watch

Watch pattern: Make a pattern for a paper watch by tracing a quarter for the watch face. Now draw a band about 1/2" wide and 2 1/2" long on each end of the watch face. (Total length of watch—about 6 1/2 inches.)

Trace the watch pattern onto **white construction paper**. Let child color the watch. After you have drawn the numbers, insert a **paper fastener** in the center of the watch face to serve as hands. One inch from one end of the band, make a slit halfway into the watchband; do the same thing at the other end except on the opposite side. Wrap the watch around child's wrist, insert the slits into one another, and secure with tape.

The watch can be a reminder that God looks after us all the time!

70 Train Picture

In advance, cut several rectangles and small circles out of **colored paper**. Show children how to **paste** several rectangles close together on a sheet of construction paper to form the train cars, using the small circles as wheels. Long strands of uncooked **spaghetti** can be glued under the train to make train tracks.

71 Birds

You'll need:

- ❑ **circles, small triangles, ovals, and strips precut from construction paper;**
- ❑ **paste; crayons; hole punch**
- ❑ **optional: small craft feathers**
- ❑ **yarn pieces 24" long**

Give each child a precut circle, triangle, and oval. Show them how to paste the three shapes together to form a bird—the oval for a body, the circle for a head, and the small triangle for a beak. Child can scribble color a bird, then draw eyes on the bird's head. For a tail, paste on strips of colored paper (or small craft feathers).

When birds are finished punch a hole in the top and loop a piece of yarn through it. Decorate the room by hanging the birds from the ceiling. The birds can be a reminder to thank God for all the good things He has made.

72 'Feather' Duster

Make a "feather" duster for helping at home. The duster may be made from a 12" length of **news-paper**. Cut in shreds to a depth of 4 inches. Roll tightly and fasten with **tape**.

This feather duster may actually be used, so let children dust the Sunday school or children's church room, or use it at home to dust their rooms.

73 House 'Rubbing'

Show children how to make a picture of a house with the texture of a building material. Have children place a piece of **typing paper** over a brick, a stucco wall, or a piece of weathered wood. **Tape** paper to the object to prevent it from moving. Children should color with the side of a **crayon** so that the texture of the material shows on the paper.

Now cut out the silhouette of a house from a sheet of **construction paper**, leaving the four sides of the construction paper as a frame. Place texture behind the frame, filling the cutout shape. **Paste** in place.

74 Sail Boat

Let each child mold a boat from **clay** or play dough. Cut one **straw** in half. Help child **tape** a triangle of **paper** to a piece of straw to make the sail. Stick the sail in the middle of the boat. Add oars to the boat by cutting the other piece of straw in half again and putting them in the boat's sides.

75 Litter Bag

Give each child a **brown lunch bag** to decorate for a litter bag. Provide large **crayons** for drawing mountains, lakes, and flowers. Or, from **magazines** cut nature pictures that can be glued on the bags.

Use the litter bag to pick up litter as you walk outdoors . . . or use it for clean-up time in the classroom . . . or suggest children keep the litter bag in the family car.

76 Thumbprint Pictures

Give each child a half sheet of light-colored **construction paper**. Press your thumb onto a **stamp pad** and make two thumbprints on the page. These prints will be the mother and father cats.

Now let each child press his or her thumb onto the stamp pad and make three or four thumbprints next to yours. Child can then draw ears, whiskers, and tails on the cats with **felt-tip pens**. Or, provide **yarn** or string to glue on the page for tails.

77 Marshmallow House

You'll need:

- ❑ **9" x 12" construction paper**
- ❑ **5" x 3" construction paper**
- ❑ **12 toothpicks; 8 miniature marshmallows**

Place each child's building materials on a 9" x 12" piece of construction paper. (The house can be carried more easily by leaving it on the sheet of construction paper.) Show how to build a foundation for the structure by joining four toothpicks and four marshmallows to form a square. Use four toothpicks to build up the walls. Then form the ceiling by adding four marshmallows and four toothpicks, forming a cube. Fold the 5" x 3" construction paper in half and set it on the structure for a roof. Use **glue** to hold in place.

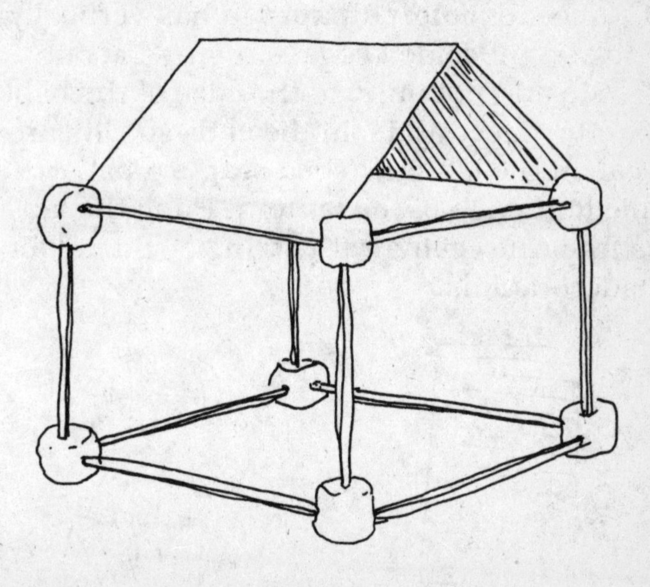

78 Butterfly

Give each child a sheet of **colored tissue paper** about 8 1/2 x 12 inches. Help child fold the paper in half horizontally.

Give each child a **twist tie** such as those included in boxes of trash bags. Place the tie around the center of the folded paper and twist once or twice tightly. The tissue paper should gather and form butterfly wings on both sides of the tie. Bend the ends of the tie to form antennae.

Decorate the wings by gluing on small pieces of brightly colored paper.

79 Japanese Lantern

Fold a sheet of **colored paper** in half vertically. Starting on the folded edge, cut strips about 1/2" wide and not quite to the edge of the paper. Unfold the paper and join the ends so slits are vertical on the lantern. Then **staple** a paper handle to the top of the lantern. Hang the lanterns from the ceiling with **string** or thread for room decorations.

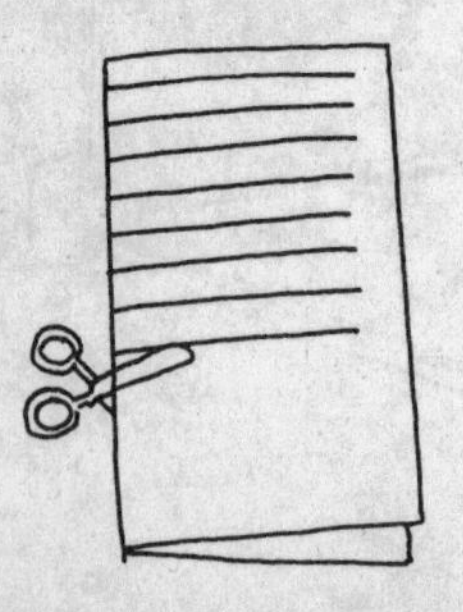

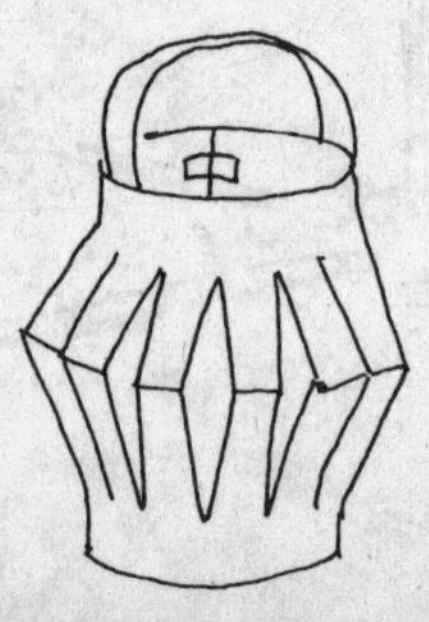

80 Mouse

You'll need:

- ❑ **construction paper**
- ❑ **cotton balls; yarn**
- ❑ **paper punch; scissors**
- ❑ **tape or glue**

In advance: For each mouse body, cut a sheet of construction paper into a large teardrop shape; also precut two rounded ears.

Give a teardrop shape to each child. The pointed end will be the mouse's nose and the rounded end will be where its tail is attached. Give each child two precut, rounded ears. Show how to paste or tape the ears to both sides of the mouse's body. With a paper punch, punch out small paper circles for eyes. Let child glue on tiny cotton ball for nose and a piece of yarn for the tail.

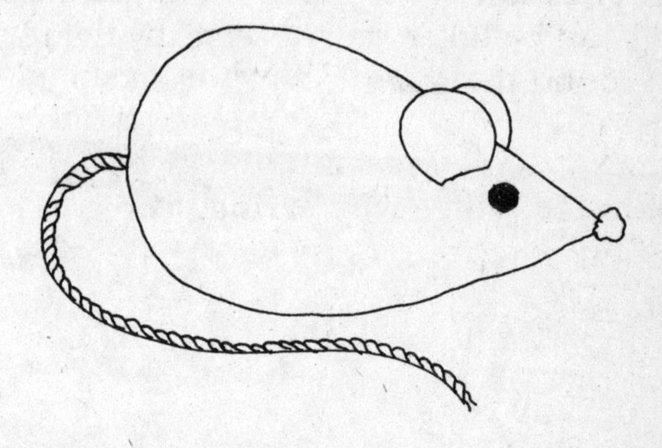

81 Ice Cream Cone

Give each child a piece of **brown construction paper** about 6" x 6" square. Roll and **tape** the square into a cone shape to resemble an ice-cream cone.

Now give each child a sheet of **tissue paper** and show how to wad it up into a ball (the "ice cream"). **Glue** or tape "ice cream" into the "cone."

82 Fish

Give each child a large sheet of **paper**. Let child tear it into a fish shape, and then scribble **color** it. With the point of a pair of **scissors**, make a small hole in the end of the fish. Put one end of a piece of **string** through the hole and tie a knot in it right in front of the hole. Now child has a fish that can be taken for a "swim" by being pulled around the room.

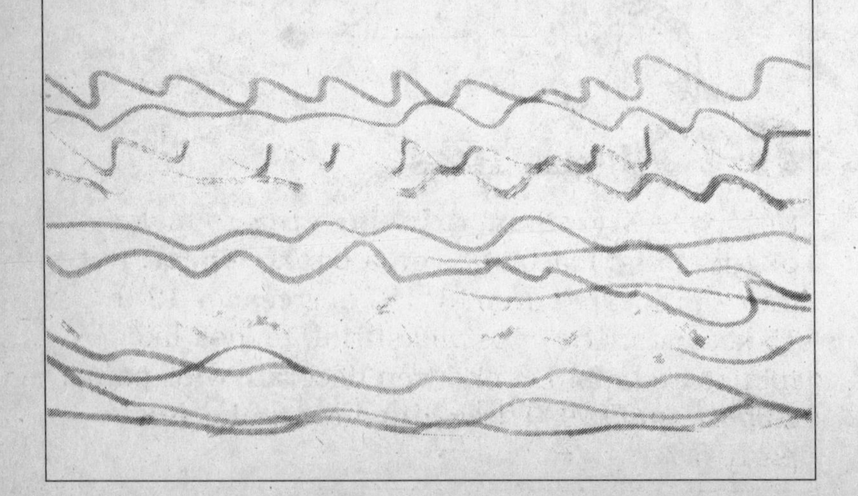

CRAFTS FOR SPECIAL DAYS

THANKSGIVING

83 Stuffed Turkeys

Draw a fat turkey body (front view) on **construction paper** and cut it out. Wad up a piece of paper and **glue** it to the back of the turkey. Place turkey on a piece of construction paper for background and glue in place. Cut feathers from construction paper and glue on background.

84 Pilgrim Hats

Use white **Styrofoam drinking cups** to make pilgrim hats. Place cups on a **cookie sheet**. Put into a preheated oven at 350 degrees for 12 to 15 seconds. The cups will shrink to look like miniature hats. Let children decorate with **paint**, **ribbon**, and **foil**. These little hats make great party favors.

85 Yarn Turkey

Draw a turkey outline about as big as your hand; make one **photocopy** for each child. Cut light and dark brown, black, and red **yarn** into various lengths to **glue** in the outline of the turkey. Longer pieces of yarn can be curved to fit. When the yarn picture is finished, cut out and glue the yarn turkey to a piece of **construction paper**.

86 Apple Turkeys

You'll need:

- ❑ **apples, raisins**
- ❑ **frosting**
- ❑ **cardboard**
- ❑ **large marshmallows**
- ❑ **toothpicks**
- ❑ **crayons or markers**

Cut a fan-shaped tail from cardboard for each turkey; let children color the tail any way they wish. Slice into apple about halfway down from the top on one side of the apple; insert tail into cut. Attach marshmallow (the head) to the other side of the apple with a toothpick. Spread frosting on the end of the marshmallow. Place raisins for the eyes, nose, and mouth in the frosting.

87 Hand-y Tree

Draw outlines of childeren's hands on **red, green, or white construction paper**. Cut out the outlines, and write a child's name on each cutout. (One child could make several.)

Make a base for the tree by rolling a large piece of flexible **cardboard** into a cone shape. Stand it upright. Starting at the bottom, **staple** or tape hand cutouts over the base. Place a star at the top and you have a holiday decoration that everyone helped make!

If you have a large group of children or would like this to be a project for the entire Sunday school, make the cone-shaped base large.

88 Memory Tree

A memory tree is a great way to remember every student you've taught. Prior to the holidays, have children cut out pretty shapes from **colored poster board** or construction paper and **paste** their school pictures on them. Using a **hole punch**, punch a hole through the picture ornament. Thread a colorful **ribbon** or piece of yarn through the hole.

A few weeks before Christmas hang the ornaments of previous classes *and* the current class on an artificial tree.

89 Christmas Place Mats

Help children trace around **Christmas cookie cutters** to make pretty designs on **red or green construction paper** for holiday place mats. Help the children attach large **star stickers** or other Christmas stickers to their place mats.

90 Play-Dough Fun

You'll need:

- ❑ **1 cup flour**
- ❑ **1/2 cup salt**
- ❑ **1 tablespoon oil**
- ❑ **dash mint extract**
- ❑ **2 teaspoons cream of tartar**
- ❑ **10 drops food coloring in 1 cup water**

Mix above ingredients in saucepan; stir and cook until mixture is the consistency of mashed potatoes and forms a ball. Knead until cool. Store in airtight container. Enough for 8 to 10 children.

Give children play dough and suggest that they make something that reminds them of the birth of Jesus. Provide **cookie cutters** to cut stars or sheep, or let children form baby Jesus, Mary, shepherds, wise men, or camels from the dough.

91 Christmas Bells

You'll need:

- ❑ **Styrofoam cups**
- ❑ **aluminum foil**
- ❑ **rickrack**
- ❑ **star stickers**
- ❑ **jingle bells (optional)**
- ❑ **glue or paste**
- ❑ **glitter**
- ❑ **chenille wires**
- ❑ **gold cord or yarn**

Turn foam cups into bells by covering them with foil or by spreading a thin coat of glue on the cups and adding rickrack and stars or by sprinkling the cups with glitter.

Use a chenille wire to make the bell clapper. Punch a hole in the top of the cup, insert the chenille wire, and make a small loop at both ends. Attach a length of gold cord or yarn in the top loop for a hanger. Or, attach a jingle bell to the chenille wire clapper so the bell will really ring.

92 Star Decoration I

Give each child a **construction paper star**. Have ready **tissue paper** cut into 1" squares. Show children how to crumple each piece of tissue paper into a little ball. Cover each star with dots of **glue**; add the tissue-paper balls to cover the star. With a **paper punch**, punch a hole in one of the points of the star. Loop a piece of **yarn** through the hole so the star may be hung up.

93 Star Decoration II

Give each child two **white paper stars** traced from a pattern. (Cut out the stars ahead of time or let children do it.) Place one star on the table in front of each child and put a dot of **glue** in the center. Place the other star on top so the points are matching, but only the centers are glued together. Help children decorate both sides of the star with **crayons** or **glitter**. Fold the points of the star away from each other so it is three-dimensional. Attach a **string** to the star between two points for hanging.

94 Christmas Story Ornaments

You'll need:

- ❑ **used Christmas cards with religious scenes**
- ❑ **lids from plastic containers**

With a **black marker**, trace a circle on each card so that when the card is trimmed the picture will fit inside a plastic lid. The edge of the lid will provide a frame. Children can choose the picture they want and cut along the black line. Help them **glue** the picture to the lid, and, with a **paper punch**, make a hole at the top of the pictures. Loop a piece of **yarn** through the hole and tie the ends.

95 Angel Decoration

You'll need:

- ❑ **8 1/2" x 11" white paper**
- ❑ **3" chenille wire**
- ❑ **small white paper circle**
- ❑ **tape**
- ❑ **glitter, yarn, trim**

Have a finished angel for children to look at as they do the project step by step.

1. A circle of white paper will be the angel's head. Add the face and hair with crayons or bits of yarn.
2. Decorate the 8 1/2" x 11" paper body of the angel with fabric trim, glitter, or crayons. Then accordion fold the body.
3. Tape the chenille wire to the head and insert between pleats at one end of the body. Press the pleats together around the chenille wire and secure with tape or staples.
4. When the pleats at the other end are fanned out the angel will stand up. You can also attach a string behind the head and form a loop to hang up each.

96 Manger Scene

You'll need:

- ❑ **plain paper cups**
- ❑ **nut cups**
- ❑ **cotton**
- ❑ **fine-point markers**
- ❑ **2 sizes small Styrofoam balls**
- ❑ **bits of dark yarn**
- ❑ **fabric scraps**
- ❑ **glue; tape**
- ❑ **sturdy cardboard**

Let each child make a different figure: Mary, Joseph, two shepherds, a sheep, baby Jesus.

For each person: Use an upside-down paper cup, with an upside-down nut cup glued on top of it. Glue dark yarn for hair and beards to foam ball; glue ball to bottom of nut cup. Draw features with fine-point markers. Use fabric scrap for Mary's head covering.

To make a sheep: Glue cotton on an upside-down nut cup. Add smallest foam ball for the head.

To make baby Jesus: Stuff cotton into nut cup; use smallest foam ball tucked into cotton for head.

Make a simple manger from cardboard. To fasten paper cup figures to the board, put a long strip of tape inside the cup so that it makes a U-shape, with the bottom of the U across the open mouth of the cup. The sides of the U adhere to the sides of the cup; the bottom of the U should fasten to the board.

97 Christmas Wreath

You'll need:

- ❑ **green posterboard**
- ❑ **red ribbon**
- ❑ **Life-Savers candy**
- ❑ **paste**

In advance: Cut out a Christmas wreath for each child. Make a pattern by cutting a small circle from the center of a larger circle. Cut the wreaths from green tagboard or heavy paper.

Let children paste candy and red ribbon bows on their wreaths.

98 Button Valentine

Each child will need a **large button** to which you have sewn a **safety pin** (leaving the point of the pin part free). Each child will also need a **construction paper heart**, a little larger than the button, on which the words "I Love You" have been printed.

To decorate: Spread a little **glue** around the outside of the heart and let the child sprinkle **glitter** on it. Child can then glue the construction paper heart to the button. When the glue is dry, pin the button on the child's coat. Some children may want to give away their buttons as valentine gifts.

99 Lily Pictures

Give each child a half piece of **construction paper** and six white, leaf-shaped petals. Show children how to roll one end of each petal around a **pencil** to make it curl. **Paste** the petals in a circle with flat ends touching and curled ends out so that the petals form a single lily. Use **crayons** to add stems and leaves.

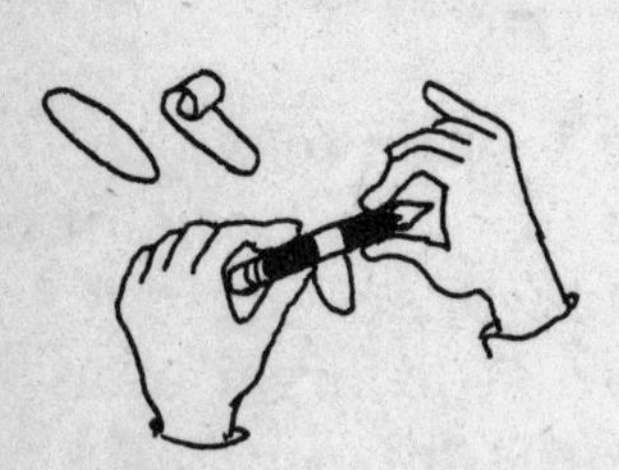

100 Tomb Picture

Give each child a **large paper plate**. Cut a straight section off the bottom so the plate is horseshoe-shape. This will represent the tomb. Draw a rectangular doorway and color the inside black. Color the rest to look like the stone tomb.

Now give each child the center circle cut from a **smaller paper plate,** large enough to cover the doorway. Attach this on the right side of the circle and doorway with a **paper fastener**.

Now child can see the tomb closed, then roll away the stone to see that the tomb is empty. Jesus is not there anymore; Jesus is alive!